This journal belongs to:

And breathe

Self-Care Journal

Suzy Reading

aster

First published in Great Britain in 2021 by Aster, an imprint of
Octopus Publishing Group Ltd
Carmelite House
50 Victoria Embankment
London EC4Y 0DZ
www.octopusbooks.co.uk

An Hachette UK Company
www.hachette.co.uk

Some of this material previously appeared in *The Self-Care Revolution*, *Self-Care for Tough Times*, *The Little Book of Self-Care* and *Stand Tall Like a Mountain*.

Distributed in the US by
Hachette Book Group
1290 Avenue of the Americas
4th and 5th Floors
New York, NY 10104

Distributed in Canada by
Canadian Manda Group
664 Annette St.
Toronto, Ontario, Canada M6S 2C8

ISBN 978-1-78325-483-5

A CIP catalogue record for this book is available from the British Library.

Printed and bound in China

10 9 8 7 6 5 4 3 2 1

Consultant Publisher: Kate Adams
Assistant Editor: Sarah Kyle
Art Director: Yasia Williams
Design: Grade Design
Production Controller: Serena Savini

CONTENTS

What is self-care?

Simply put, self-care is nourishment for the head, the heart and the body. I always say that self-care is healthcare – because without our health, what do we have? By 'health', I am referring to physical health, emotional health, energetic health and mental health. If it's OK to brush your teeth and hit the gym, it is equally OK to give yourself permission to stop, rest and top up your energy bank. I urge you to take a look at your self-care practices and make sure there is something in there for every aspect of your well-being: mind and body.

Please don't equate self-care with pampering: it *can* be pampering, but it is not limited to luxurious practices. Sometimes, a restorative act is just what you need; in other moments, the true act of self-care might be the last thing you actually *feel* like doing, something that challenges you or requires you to step up, like sitting to meditate when your mind is whirring, or heading out for a jog when the sofa is calling to you.

To make it easier to understand self-care, there is a second part to my definition. Self-care is nourishing yourself in this moment AND nourishing the person you are becoming. If you're not sure, ask your 'Future Self'. There is great wisdom to be mined there. The manner of asking will vary from person to person – and, for you, from moment to moment – but this definition and a varied toolkit will serve you well.

What does self-care mean to you?

The benefits of self-care

- Self-care helps us cope in the moment, whether we're rising to meet a work challenge or digging deep to meet our children's needs. Self-care helps us navigate these experiences with a sense of calm, poise and purpose.

- After periods of stress, loss, conflict or change, self-care can also put us back together. We all need a toolkit to help us restore, replenish and heal, because no one is immune from these experiences.

- Engaging in proactive self-care helps to boost our resilience, providing us with a protective buffer against future challenges. Just like a car needs fuel to move, we need energy to get through our day, and the greater the reserves in our energy bank, the more effective we are. An act of self-care is like a deposit in our energy bank. We need a healthy balance in our bank because it's not just crisis and illness that deplete us; things we desperately want – like promotions, having kids, getting married, buying or renovating a house or just planning a holiday – have an energetic tax on us too! Self-care allows us to keep giving and keep going. Energetic bankruptcy serves no one.

- And, last but not least, self-care gives us access to our best selves. Think of any goal or quality you aspire to possess – you are more likely to achieve it when you are well nourished. Self-care helps us all become kinder, more compassionate people and this benefits everyone whose lives we touch.

How could practising a little more self-care benefit you?

_____

_____

_____

_____

_____

_____

_____

_____

_____

_____

_____

_____

_____

_____

_____

How to use this journal and how it works

We all know broadly what we need to do to feel energetic and healthy. The purpose of this journal is to help you get clear on what this means to you.

Use this journal daily and, in as little as five minutes, it will bring a sense of fresh purpose and zest to your day. Achievable and sustainable change is best created in small increments, so every time you check in with this journal, there is the opportunity to reaffirm your commitment to your healthy habits and to embark on a new wave of change once each habit is integrated into your everyday life.

Start by 'connecting with your why' in the following pages, using the prompts to identify the scaffolding in life that you need in order to flourish. Celebrate what you are already doing well, acknowledge what needs some tweaking and use the goal-setting chapter to break it down into mini actionable steps.

Draw practical inspiration from the other chapters on how to boost your well-being, going straight to wherever you feel drawn. Work on that aspect of your health, and keep returning to your journal to build your self-insight and motivation, and to grow your self-care toolkit.

CONNECT WITH YOUR 'WHY'

Take a moment to connect with your personal 'why' of self-care. This is the stuff that will truly free you and motivate you to take alternative action – because if you want to feel differently, you've got to do things differently. It's not enough just to think about it.

1. Think about one role in life that feels really important to you. It could be partner, parent, carer, business owner or practitioner. Reflect on the kind of qualities you aspire to possess in this role. How do you want to be experienced by others? What kind of behaviour and values do you want to model? What kind of legacy would you like to leave behind?

2. Now jot down the kind of scaffolding you need in life in order to be this version of you, being as specific as you can, from morning through till evening. What are the non-negotiables in everyday life necessary for you to be able to function in this way?

3. Based on your reflections to the prompts above, write down what self-care facilitates in your life, for you and your loved ones. Write down why it's not only OK but necessary to practise self-care. Return to this list whenever guilt gets in the way, or if you feel as if you don't deserve to feel better.

The vitality wheel

I created the 'vitality wheel' as a simple method of communicating the different ways in which you can make a deposit into your energy bank. The goal of the vitality wheel is to empower you to better care for yourself. In one simple diagram, you can be reminded of eight different avenues of nourishment.

In this journal, there are prompts to encourage reflection, enquiry and action in the eight areas of the vitality wheel. I would encourage you to start with Values & Purpose and Goal-Setting, and then explore the other areas that speak to you most, whether that's having a more positive relationship with Sleep, Rest & Relaxation, firing up your motivation for Movement & Nutrition, or developing Coping Skills for the more challenging times in life.

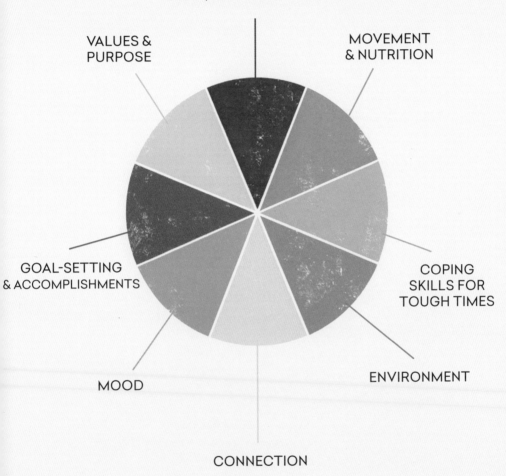

SLEEP, REST & RELAXATION

MOVEMENT & NUTRITION

VALUES & PURPOSE

COPING SKILLS FOR TOUGH TIMES

GOAL-SETTING & ACCOMPLISHMENTS

ENVIRONMENT

MOOD

CONNECTION

Practices

I have included a few self-care practices that only take moments or minutes. As you try these practices, check in with yourself and notice how you feel before and after. This helps us build our mindfulness muscles.

To deepen your awareness of your physical body, having a broad vocabulary of physical sensations will help. Ponder these words a while and refer to this list while you are engaging in a mindful check-in or during your yoga:

Sharp, dull, radiating, pulsing, shooting, throbbing, fizzing, pins and needles, warm, cold, tight, loose, stringy, achy, heavy, light, constricted, loose, open, spacious, expansive, faint, goosebumps, fluid, stuck, frozen, numb, zingy, floppy, puffy, jittery, fuzzy, twitchy, shivers, tingling, trembling, dense, faint, dizzy, bloated, smooth, soft, energized.

Where do you notice these sensations, and do they change with time? Is there some kind of message in them? Are they suggesting to you any kind of movement in response? There is no right or wrong: just let curiosity guide you.

These and other practices are perfect for dotting throughout your day. As you build your self-awareness through self-care, identify useful opportunities to use these practices. Self-insight, compassion and healthy habits come together in these micro-moments of nourishment.

Mountain breath

This is an excellent practice for energizing your body and mind in the morning or whenever you need a boost during the day.

Stand tall with your feet hip width apart. As you breathe in, reach your arms out wide and up overhead, palms touching. Look up to lift your mood.

As you exhale, bring your hands down through the centre line of your body, in prayer position, bringing the energy towards your heart. Repeat six times.

VALUES & PURPOSE
GETTING TO KNOW YOURSELF

Your values lie at the heart of why you engage in self-care. By committing to regular self-care, you are in the best possible place to live the life that you aspire to lead and to become the person you aspire to be. Self-care is a dual feedback loop – you engage in self-care to fully live your values, and articulating your values will motivate you to commit to self-care.

Connecting with your purpose can transform how you feel about an activity, your role in life or your circumstances. When you evaluate your choices in light of what takes you towards or away from your values, it gives you clarity on which the right path of action, and decision-making gets easier. It's not enough to know what you want in life – you've got to know why you want it. Being really crystal clear on why you are taking a particular course of action galvanizes you to keep going when life tests you.

Describe yourself when you are well-nourished and topped up with energy. What does this facilitate in your life? What does this allow you to do or be?

_____

_____

_____

_____

_____

_____

_____

_____

_____

_____

_____

_____

_____

_____

Describe yourself when you are depleted, empty or fatigued. How does this affect your life and the people around you?

_____

_____

_____

_____

_____

_____

_____

_____

_____

_____

_____

_____

_____

_____

_____

_____

_____

Current choices

Part of getting to know yourself is identifying your current choices, in order to establish a baseline and to acknowledge the impact of what you're doing now... this is all helpful for motivating change. Taking stock and noticing the choices you are currently making will help you identify any changes you want to make.

1. What are the things you are turning to right now for comfort and support? Are they genuinely tending to your needs in the moment and are they nurturing your future self? At what cost do you keep using these coping mechanisms?

2. Are there some soothing pursuits you used to enjoy that you've forgotten about? Is there something you would like to reclaim? Maybe you'd like to pick up your guitar again – or is there a place you'd like to go and sit to feel connected with someone? Perhaps you'd like to return to something, but it needs to take a different shape now because your life has changed. How can you dip into it in a way that honours where you are at right now? If you can't think of a way on your own, sit down with a friend and see if you can find one together, or think of something new that helps you meet that need.

3. Thinking of self-care as energy management, give yourself permission to guard your precious energy bank. Are there energy-zappers that you can eliminate, avoid or minimize? Identify those people, places or tasks that deplete you and think of steps you can take to protect yourself. If these energy-zappers are unavoidable, use this book to top up your energy bank in compensation.

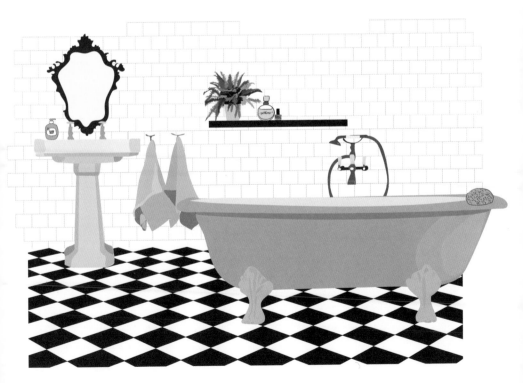

WHAT CAN YOU SWAP?

Often when we feel squeezed by life, we turn to caffeine to get us going, screens to occupy us or distract us from our feelings, food for comfort, online shopping for a feel-good buzz and alcohol to calm us down.

While all of these things may help us cope in the moment, they tend to have an energetic tax, creating mind fog, the jitters, diminishing our self-esteem, adding to our financial burden or scuppering our ability to sleep. In short, they might help us cope today but they make tomorrow harder. Now, I don't aspire to lead a life devoid of chocolate, red wine and Netflix, but if we habitually turn to these things, they deplete us and make life tougher.

Spend some time thinking about life-giving alternatives to these crutches. There is an underlying need that still has to be met, but we can make a choice our future selves will thank us for. Here are some examples:

- Practise 'mountain breaths' (see page 17) instead of drinking another cup of coffee.

- Call a buddy rather than scrolling.

- Use scent rather than comfort food.

- Try doing 'legs up the wall' (see page 90) rather than drinking wine.

- Dig out an item of clothing or a product you love and already own rather than buying more.

IDENTIFY YOUR STRENGTHS & VALUES

Your strengths are things you do well naturally and effortlessly, and your values are whatever matters most to you. They both light us up and motivate us. We feel powerful when we put our strengths to good use and we can call on them to help us navigate tough situations. Knowing our values helps us connect with a sense of meaning in challenging times.

Play with the following questions to gain greater self-insight:

Who do you feel a resonance or connection with? Why?

_____

_____

_____

_____

Who do you admire and why? These can be people in your life, celebrities, historical figures or even fictional characters.

_____

_____

_____

_____

What are your proudest moments, and why? What qualities did you draw on in these moments?

_____

_____

_____

_____

If money was no issue, how would you spend your time?

_____

_____

_____

_____

If you had nothing to fear, what action would you take, or what would you stop doing?

_____

_____

_____

_____

Reflect on what makes you angry. What underlying morals are being impinged on in this situation?

_____

_____

_____

_____

What's on your bucket list?

Have you ever made a list of all the precious things you'd like to achieve or experience? Asking yourself why you want these things can be fertile ground for articulating what's most important to you. Or ponder this prompt: 'If I had thirty days to live, I would...' to crystallize what it is you hold dear in life.

If I had thirty days to live, I would...

_____

_____

_____

_____

_____

_____

_____

_____

_____

_____

_____

_____

_____

_____

_____

_____

_____

_____

_____

WHAT IS MEANINGFUL IN THE DIFFERENT ASPECTS OF YOUR LIFE?

- Are you living your truth?

- Are you living a life imbued with personal meaning?

- Are you living a life inspired by your own unique strengths, gifts and talents?

- Are you living a life guided and shaped by your own personal values?

Set your intention

Identify a value or a personal strength and set the intention to use it today. Think along the lines of a quality that's important to you or one that comes naturally to you, such as kindness, fairness, courage, compassion or zest. Throughout your day, look for opportunities to bring this quality into action, feeling how the congruence with your values and strengths boosts your mood, your self-confidence and your sense of peace. This practice helps you switch off autopilot and take more purposeful action. Even just the practice of articulating your strengths and values can be uplifting.

Reflect on how this practice affected your day. What quality did you choose?

_____

_____

_____

_____

_____

_____

_____

_____

_____

_____

_____

_____

_____

_____

_____

MAKE A LIFE MAP

This exercise is a visual tool and you can get as creative as you like with it. Start by mapping out different areas of your life that are important to you. This will be different for everyone, but some suggestions might be: family, love or relationships, work, study, personal growth, leisure, learning, social connection, household, community, health, downtime, finances and spirituality.

Represent these however you like, with text or shapes. Use colour and highlight the things that require your attention. Jot down worries or fears, if you like. Observe the areas of life in which you're functioning well – express a feeling of thankfulness and give yourself a pat on the back for your accomplishments there.

Identify where your sources of stress or depletion lie and mark these on your map, bringing them to the light.

Look over your map, and if you spot any problems that don't belong to you, or worries that you can drop, relish crossing these out.

GOAL-SETTING & ACCOMPLISHMENTS

If you want to achieve any kind of change in life, whether that be integrating a new healthy habit, getting back on your feet after adversity, or making a bold career move, setting a goal will help you take action. Research clearly shows you are more likely to make something happen if you set yourself a goal around it. Goals help to structure your time and give shape to your life. They fine-tune your awareness, give you a sense of drive and staying power, and help you take action consistent with your values. Research also shows that people who have a commitment to something personally significant are happier than those without firm aspirations.

If the thought of setting goals leaves you feeling cold, hold on. There are some really simple goal-setting principles that could transform how you feel about goals and how effective they can be. While the right goals uplift you, poorly crafted goals can demotivate you. Before you set any goals, be honest with yourself about your energy levels and the demands you are facing already in life right now. I often hear people say they just don't have time to set goals. If you fall into this camp, then my cautionary words would be that if you want to create any meaningful shift, it is unlikely to happen on its own. Having a goal will help you grow.

WHAT WOULD YOU LIKE TO CULTIVATE MORE OF AND WHY?

The best goals are set in service of your values, because it is that sense of 'why' that will see you through.

What would you like to cultivate more of in your life?

_____

_____

_____

_____

_____

_____

_____

What do you stand to lose if you don't do it?

_____

_____

_____

_____

_____

_____

_____

_____

What will cultivating it allow you to do?

_____

_____

_____

_____

_____

_____

_____

_____

_____

_____

_____

_____

_____

_____

_____

_____

_____

Time for reflection

Think about one goal you set for yourself in the past that you didn't achieve. Without self-flagellation – permission to be human here – ask yourself what happened? Why didn't this goal come through for you? Was it timing? Was it access to resources? Was it a lack of knowledge? Was this goal something you really cared about, or was it something someone else wanted for you? What external factors made it hard?

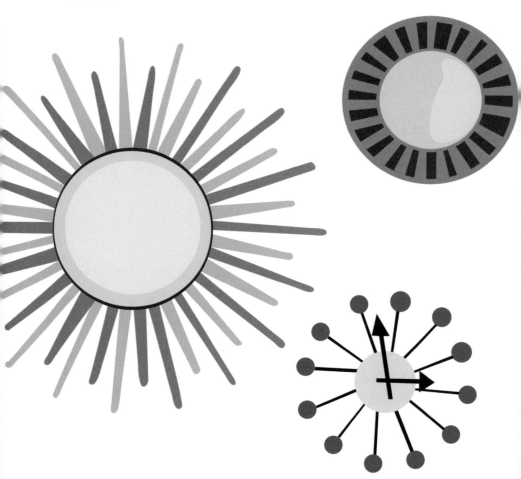

Think about one goal you set for yourself in the past that you DID achieve. Reflect on how you managed to achieve it. What did it mean to you, and what did you do? Observe the differences between the two goals and the differences in the actions you took towards them. What can you learn about goal-setting or about yourself from these reflections?

_____

_____

_____

_____

_____

_____

_____

_____

_____

_____

_____

Identify your goals

The clearer and more specific your goals, the better, and it's also hepful give them a loose timeframe. The act of recording your goals is an important step in making a psychological contract with yourself. Once you've chosen your goals mindfully (you'll know your goals are right for you if thinking about them stimulates a feeling of excitement or positivity), you then need to consider some actionable steps. It's not enough just to think about your goals; to achieve any change, you have to take action.

Use this checklist to help identify your goals:

Intrinsic – Your goals should be that are personally rewarding and inspiring to you as opposed to 'extrinsic' goals, which tend to be a reflection of what other people want for you or what you think you 'should' do. These are goals that have been imposed on you.

Authentic – They should be goals anchored in your own values, interests and beliefs, and should fit well with your personality and natural strengths.

'Approach' rather than 'avoid' – Frame your goals positively so that they involve becoming or approaching a desirable outcome rather than avoiding an undesirable outcome. Your goals act as powerful primer statements to your brain, so a goal to 'eat less chocolate' will have your brain focusing on... chocolate! A more effective goal would be to carve a new ritual of pleasure, such as a savoured cup of tea. In my experience, when we shift the goal from something like 'lose weight', to 'daily self-care to boost vitality', we start getting into great shape and making better lifestyle choices naturally.

Harmonious – Make sure that your goals complement each other rather than conflict with each other. Competing goals are a recipe for inner conflict and might make you feel stuck in the middle! It helps to zoom out and be honest with yourself about what is reasonable and achievable right now.

Reasonable and flexible – Take into account your current circumstances and available resources. These variables can change, so you need to keep your goal-setting fluid. Rigid goals create another recipe for inner conflict, so remember to allow some wiggle room for your evolving circumstances.

Break it down

Once you've worked out what you want, you need to work out how you're going to do it. Think about the actions or behaviours required to move you towards your goal. For example, if your goal is to boost your physical fitness, what specific action does this require? What do you need to do more of or what new behaviours do you need to engage in to bring your goal to life?

Write down three actionable steps you can take now to progress you towards achieving your goal.

_____

_____

_____

_____

_____

_____

_____

_____

_____

_____

_____

_____

_____

_____

_____

_____

OVERCOMING OBSTACLES

What obstacles might get in the way of your progress towards your goals, and how can you overcome each of these? How can you use your strengths to look at these obstacles?

Primer statements can be useful in navigating these curveballs. For example:

- If I have to work late and miss my gym class, then I will do my ten-minute home workout routine.

- If I don't have time to meditate, I will listen to yoga nidra as I drop off at night.

- If I don't have the energy to go for that planned jog, I will go for a walk.

- If I don't have time to stop and rest, I will take three breaths to refresh.

Mindful ritual

Come into a seated position and ease out any tension in your neck, chest and upper back with some shoulder rolls and head turns (see pages 50–51).

Drop the weight of your day from your shoulders and take a few relaxed breaths. Form a steeple shape with your hands by gently spreading your fingertips wide and touching the tip of each finger and thumb together at chest height in front of your body. Feel the pulse of your fingertips and the warmth there, noticing how this gesture brings you a real presence of mind.

Next, notice how the elevation of your fingertips is echoed by the structure of your mouth. Press the tip of your tongue to the roof of your mouth, feeling how the upper palate is like the steeple lifting skywards. There is a poise and peace here.

Repeat the words: 'I am the architect of my life,' and breathe life and belief into this statement.

A ritual of soothing touch

Touch, whether received from another or self-administered, releases oxytocin. Oxytocin is a stress-managing hormone, and is critical to a sense of feeling safe. It facilitates social bonds, love and belonging, resilience and stress-buffering, allowing the body to adapt and heal in response to stress.

Drawing on the power of touch, this face, head, neck and shoulder practice has a deeply restorative effect.

Check in and notice how you feel before trying this practice, observing your breathing, your levels of tension, the quality of your thoughts, and your mood. Engage in the practice or just part of it and note down any changes in how you feel afterwards.

Shoulder rub – Lay your right hand across your left shoulder beside your neck. Press your fingertips in and draw them across the ridge of your shoulder. Repeat this six times, moving further away from your neck with each repetition. Repeat on the other side.

Head turns – Relax your arms by your sides and keep your shoulders away from your ears. Keeping your chin parallel to the ground, look to the right, then look to your left. Do this three times each way, lubricating the neck.

Shoulder roll – Lay your fingertips on your shoulders. As you breathe in, bring your elbows forwards and upwards, and as you exhale, take them back and down. Repeat six times. Feel how this frees your chest and shoulders and lifts you into a more upright posture.

Cup your face – Rest your chin in your hands and wrap your fingertips around your face, up to your temples. Hold here for six calm breaths.

Bathe your eyes – Rub your hands together to create warmth, then cup your palms over your eyes, extending tenderness toward yourself for six breaths.

Recognize your accomplishments

There is such a source of energy and sustenance available to you in recognizing your own achievements. Reflecting on what is going well is a powerful way to boost your sense of self-worth. This is not just about public accolades and the big things like graduations – it is about noticing a job well done on an everyday level.

Be on the lookout for your accomplishments, small and large. Reflect on the effort you've put in to make them happen and savour that achievement. Feel how the act of noticing your accomplishments fills your cup! Don't just wait for others to say 'well done': you can do it for yourself, and it can feel just as satisfying.

CONNECTION

There is no denying the profound effect that social connection, or its absence, has on our well-being. Humans have a basic need to belong – it is an evolutionary, biological drive. Our relationships provide us with support in times of crisis, and they amplify our joy in the good times. In connecting with others, we experience love, comfort and acceptance, adding meaning and purpose to our lives. Connection sets into motion that upward spiral of positivity: the more time, energy and effort we put into building more positive connections, the more we experience joyful emotions.

Investing in social connection is one of the most powerful self-care strategies for boosting your well-being.

Who's on your team?

I like to think I have a whole team of people on my side. Who's on yours? This is worth reflecting on and taking a moment to write it down. Who do you share the journey with and who are the people or practitioners that help put you back together when crisis hits? What do you value about each person? What strengths do they possess?

Help with reaching your goals

Connecting with other people is deeply nourishing, whether they are close friends or strangers. It provides us with a sense of shared experience, common humanity and belonging, all of which feed the soul.

Are there people on your team, or who you can connect with, who can be part of your journey towards reaching your goals? How can they help you take action? Even if you don't share the same goal, can you support each other in the pursuit of your individual goals? Try keeping each other accountable and motivated along the way.

Reaching out

Think about all the people who are in your corner, willing you on. Sometimes we hesitate to reach out, feeling it's not OK to ask for help. Sometimes help is offered, but it's not what we need. Give yourself permission not only to ask for help but to shape how that help is given. Think about how you've felt in the past towards a friend having a tough time. I'm sure you were just waiting to lend a hand, often not knowing how best to be of support. Rather than being a burden, you can actually do people a great service by reaching out to them for help – it feels good being helpful and it deepens your bonds! It's also important to consider that not everyone will be able to give you the kind of help you need (it's not a lack of love!), so choose wisely and draw on the strengths of the people around you. If you need a kind ear, turn to the person who loves giving that, not the problem-solver who specializes in coming up with a list of things you could do. Different people in different moments will help you through.

Make a list of all the people on your team and what you appreciate about them. In tough moments, imagine them with you, wrapping you up in their love.

_____

_____

_____

_____

_____

_____

_____

_____

_____

_____

_____

_____

_____

_____

_____

_____

_____

MOOD

You might think that self-care is designed to help you feel happy all the time, but the reality is that it's much more important to acknowledge how you feel and develop your self-awareness. Your mood might be affected by many factors, including whether your energy bank is nicely topped up or running on empty, and your ability to dial down your inner critic and be kind to yourself.

Noticing how you are: 'I am. I can'

If you're feeling flustered, repeat this mantra to find peace and clarity. It will help you break things down into manageable steps and galvanize you to beat overwhelm.

The first part, 'I am', allows you to own how you feel right now, and to channel how you'd like to feel. The 'I can' part encourages you to focus on what lies within your control. I like to draw on the 'I can' to remind me of a strength that will help me step up to meet the demands of the situation.

So, for example: I am nervous right now but I know this feeling will pass, and I can soothe myself with kind words (see page 70), tender touch (see page 51) and some calming breaths (see page 82).

Feeling your feelings

Normal psychological functioning is not an absence of unpleasant feelings! Being resilient doesn't make us immune to stress, worry or grief. The normal response to tough times is to struggle.

It is totally normal to experience anxious or depressed thinking at times. They are just thoughts, and it doesn't necessarily follow that you are 'anxious' or 'depressed'. So, here is the life-changing bit – it's OK to stop trying to eradicate negative thoughts and feelings!

We're not aiming for happiness all the time; we're aiming for an emotional response appropriate to the situation and one that will help us achieve our desired outcome. All emotions have their place. In fact I no longer use the distinction of positive or negative emotions. Anger might not feel nice, but it helps us protect ourselves and stand up for our beliefs. Grief might be painful, but it's the natural response to loss, and, like sadness, is a call to us to contemplate, slow down and to conserve our energy.

Embarrassment is a signal that we've made an error and that some kind of correction is needed. Guilt suggests we've broken our moral code and we need to adjust our behaviour. Doubt prompts us to assess our skills. None of these feelings are particularly comfortable, but they have their healthy place and purpose.

What emotions are present for you right now – are they appropriate to the situation, and are you feeling them at the appropriate intensity? Are they helping or hindering you in reaching your desired outcome? What messages do your emotions have for you – is there something you feel you need to do in response?

_____

_____

_____

_____

_____

_____

_____

_____

_____

_____

Understanding your emotions

Language creates a link between experience and thought, so in order to make sense of your emotions, you need the vocabularly to describe and categorize them. Having the words to label our emotions helps us develop 'emotional literacy', and being able to describe the breadth of experience of different emotions is called 'emotional granularity'. Rather than just feeling 'bad', being able to describe the shades of different feelings like boredom, frustration or disappointment helps us take more targeted action and move through these feelings.

Take in this list of different emotions. Look up the definition of any you are unsure of. What might their purpose be? Are there some that you try to avoid? Why might this be? How would it be if you made space for these emotions?

Love *Courage* **Admiration** *Power*

Joy *Playfulness* **Awe** Zest

Bliss **Gratitude**

Vigilance Remorse **Annoyance** Gloom

Elation **Contentment** *Rage*

Inspiration Happiness

Openness **Hope** Eagerness

Amazement Astonishment

Shock Fear **Worry** Anxiety **Disgust**

Peace **Relaxation** Serenity

Pride *Excitement* Anticipation *Boredom*

Acceptance **Interest** Apathy **Dismay** Amusement
Curiosity Sadness **Tetchiness**

Nervousness *Melancholy*

Irritation Alarm **Anger**

Mortification Unease

Rejection Embarrassment

Resentment Envy **Jealousy** Disappointment
Loneliness **Guilt**

Jaw sequence

We hold a great deal of tension in our jaws, clenching our teeth as we muscle our way through difficult experiences, or 'biting our lips' to suppress emotions. Use this sequence to let go of the things you haven't said.

1. Circle your bottom jaw around your top front teeth. Do this six times one way, then change direction.

2. Move your bottom jaw in a circle as if you are drawing the letter 'O'. Do this six times in each direction.

3. This one is harder: take your bottom jaw upwards and forwards and then down and back. Then reverse it, taking your bottom jaw forwards and up, and then back and down. It's like an elliptical action. Do this six times each way.

4. Massage your jaw with a gentle downwards stroke a few times and notice how much more relaxed your face feels now.

Lion breath

Sometimes we need to expunge ourselves of big emotions like anger, resentment and frustration. The challenge is to do this in ways that are not harmful. Roaring it out in lion breath can help: it's akin to screaming into a pillow. Breathe in through your nose, then exhale with an explosive 'ha' sound through your mouth, sticking your tongue out as far as possible, three times. Blow away what is hard or harmful to say.

Without judgement, note down how you feel before these practices, paying attention to the presence of any emotions, thoughts or sensations. Observe any feelings that arise during each practice and see how you feel after them, jotting down any changes or insights.

_____

_____

_____

_____

_____

_____

_____

_____

_____

_____

_____

_____

_____

Kinder self-talk

Today, every time your inner critic pops up or you face a challenge, try tuning into your inner cheerleader – yes, you have one! Your inner critic might feel more familiar, but I promise you, your inner cheerleader is just waiting to be heard. If you're having a tough moment, pause and ask yourself: how would anyone feel if they were in your shoes? How can you encourage yourself as you would a buddy in this moment? What might you say to someone else in these circumstances?

What personal strengths can you draw upon to help you right now? Your inner cheerleader will remind you and will help you recognize the right action to take. There's no merit or benefit in indulging your inner critic, but don't bother trying to silence that voice either. In my experience, trying to stamp it out just makes it louder. Remember, it's just a thought, not your identity or some prophecy of the future. Instead, let your inner cheerleader get a look in. Practise the skill of offering yourself a supportive and kind word, and you'll see that great things truly blossom from self-compassion.

What is my inner cheerleader telling me today?

_____

_____

_____

_____

_____

_____

_____

_____

_____

_____

_____

_____

_____

_____

_____

Filling your cup – what are your mood-boosters?

Take stock of your day and observe the things that naturally top up your energy. Try to do more of these things. These mood-boosting activities could include taking a walk in nature, listening to music, painting, enjoying movement, indulging in scent, playing with your dog, watching online cat videos or tuning into your favourite podcast

Notice, as well, the things that tend to deplete you. Some of these things are unavoidable, and in those circumstances we use self-care to make up for the deficit. You may, however, find there are some things that you can minimize or avoid altogether – please give yourself the permission to make these choices and take care of your energy bank balance.

My mood-boosters...

_____

_____

_____

_____

_____

_____

_____

_____

_____

_____

_____

_____

_____

_____

_____

_____

GRATITUDE

End the day on a positive note. Try the exercise Martin Seligman calls 'The Three Blessings'. Write down three positive things that happened in your day – and, importantly, *why* they happened.

For example, I'm grateful for getting a call from my friend today. Why did it happen? Because we care about each other and we have a strong bond. The underlying reasons help us feel a sense of peace and optimism.

There is no right or wrong here: write down whatever comes to mind. Notice how this changes the quality of your mood and helps focus your mind on more constructive thoughts.

A positive thing that happened today...

_____

_____

Why it happened...

_____

_____

A positive thing that happened today...

_____

_____

Why it happened...

_____

_____

A positive thing that happened today...

_____

_____

Why it happened...

_____

_____

I wonder...

Curiosity is a powerful mood alchemist. It frees up stuck, rigid thinking, giving us space to respond to situations with greater care and compassion. Developing the skill of curiosity helps us to see things from different perspectives and take things less personally.

To cultivate curiosity, try this simple practice: when you face minor irritations in your day, use the phrase 'I wonder...' For example, see if you can generate different, maybe more charitable, explanations for the behaviour of other people. Ask yourself what might lie beneath the actions of others and consider the wide range of ways someone else might be feeling.

Using the phrase 'I wonder...' will help you question assumptions or conclusions that you've leaped to. Even just taking the time to think about a range of possible explanations gives you a chance to cool off and choose more mindfully how you'll respond.

Reflect on how this practice went. Did you discover some alternative ways to look at certain situations and consider the other factors at play?

_____

_____

_____

_____

_____

_____

_____

_____

_____

_____

_____

_____

_____

_____

Savouring

This is one of my all-time favourite mood-boosters. Get good at savouring and you will have instant access to positivity. Savouring can be described as thoughts or actions that create, amplify and sustain enjoyment. This is where you notice a pleasurable experience, give it your full attention, and immerse yourself in all the enjoyable things about it, feeling it as intensely as you can and letting the experience linger for as long as possible.

There are three different components to savouring – past, present and future. You can savour the past by reminiscing with a buddy over a shared happy memory. You can savour the present by immersing yourself in the pleasure of the moment at hand, like a good cup of coffee, feeling its warming effects, taste and aroma. You can savour the future by joyfully anticipating and visualizing what might lie ahead, like that long-awaited summer holiday. Cultivate this fantastic skill of savouring and don't let a moment of joy escape you!

Make a 'memory bank'. Record a
pleasurable experience here in your journal.
Get as descriptive as you can about how
it made you feel in terms of thoughts,
emotions and sensations.

_____

_____

_____

_____

_____

_____

_____

_____

_____

_____

_____

_____

_____

SLEEP, REST & RELAXATION

How is your relationship with sleep and rest? What messaging have you taken on? Is it OK to rest? What was modelled for you growing up? Do those scripts need some rewriting?

During and after times of upheaval, our bodies are flooded with stress hormones that can leave us feeling depleted, anxious and depressed. The sympathetic nervous system has been sent into overdrive, and that chronic experience of 'fight or flight' can make you feel like you've been hit by a truck. We need to stimulate the parasympathetic nervous system (PNS) – the part that is responsible for the 'rest and digest' functions of the body – in order to mediate the effects of these stress hormones. The best way to promote the PNS is to get adequate sleep, make time for rest and relaxation and return to a more natural, relaxed and expansive way of breathing.

Back to the breath

Find a seated position that allows you to elongate your spine and sit comfortably for a few minutes. This could be cross-legged on the floor, with a bolster beneath your sit bones, or in a chair. Be guided by your comfort.

Feel the support of the floor or chair beneath you and encourage the crown of your head to snake its way skyward, feeling the buoyancy of your skull. Soften all the muscles of your face, close your eyes, release your jaw and loosen your tongue in your mouth. Let your shoulders drop heavily away from your ears. Spend a minute noticing how it feels to sit still, allowing the thoughts and feelings to pop up as they will.

Now direct your attention to your breathing. There is no right way to breathe, and this is not thinking about the breath – this is feeling the sensations of it. Let your breath be exactly as you find it, noticing where you feel it move through your body. It could be your tummy, your sides, your back, your chest and even up into your collarbones. Let it move through you, filling all the internal nooks and crannies on the inhalation, and feeling just a gentle, effortless retraction back to your centre on the exhalation.

Now draw attention to the position you've chosen for your hands. Just notice how pleasant it feels for the hands to have nothing to do. Next, place your hand flat down on your thighs with your palms facing down in a way that keeps your shoulders relaxed and allows you to soften the whole length of your arm. Get curious about the effect this hand mudra has on your breathing. What you might notice is that it makes your exhalation longer, deeper or easier. Enjoy ten soothing breaths with the palms facing downwards, creating a feeling of grounding and stability.

Next, turn your palms to face upwards and allow your fingertips to curl loosely toward your palms. Notice how this hand gesture changes the sensation of your breathing. You might begin to feel the inhalation seems lighter, longer or easier. Savour ten smooth breaths with your palms facing upwards, experiencing a sense of openness, being invigorated with fresh energy.

Lastly, bring the tip of the thumb and first finger of each hand together to touch in chin mudra. Observe how this hand position changes your breathing. You may feel this directs your breath into your abdomen, encouraging diaphragmatic breathing, which is naturally calming and centring. Be here for another ten breaths (or longer if it feels good) or return to the hand position that resonates with you most, anchoring your mind on the sensation of your breath. Every time your mind wanders elsewhere, without criticism, bring it back to your breath.

How is your sleep?

What is a good night's sleep?

Good sleep doesn't need to be in one unbroken stretch. Throughout most of human history (until the advent of artificial light) sleep was divided into two separate periods with a wakeful period in between, rather than the revered uninterrupted stretch to which we now aspire, so segmented sleep is very normal. This period of wakefulness, which might have lasted a few hours, was historically used as a time for self-reflection, prayer, meditation, reading, writing and sex. The night-time wakefulness that some of us experience now might just be a natural expression of our pre-industrial sleeping patterns. What's important is getting sufficient time in bed to meet your sleep needs, and having a toolkit of calming practices that help you rest and make peace with wakefulness.

What puts us to sleep?

There are two main ways in which your body puts you to sleep, and knowing these mechanisms helps you make choices more conducive to better sleep. Sleeping and waking cycles are guided by the circadian rhythm – your master clock – which is individual to you. Long-haul travel interrupts this, as does the blue light emitted from screens, which suppresses melatonin production. Getting plenty of natural light in the morning can combat the effects of being in front of a screen during the working day.

The other mechanism is sleep pressure, which builds up as you stay awake and releases when you go to bed. This explains why falling asleep on the sofa at 9pm can scupper your sleep when you finally make it to bed. Well-timed naps, on the other hand, can promote better sleep at night.

Are you getting enough sleep?

Surviving on too little sleep is not a badge of honour: most adults need seven to nine hours. You may get by on less, but for how long and at what cost? Sleep needs are individual, so get to know how many hours you personally need to function well and make sleep a genuine priority. If you find yourself madly rushing about trying to get things done at night at the expense of time in bed, ask yourself: 'Does this really need to be done right now?' Zoning out in front of the TV is not as relaxing as getting the sleep you need.

How many hours of sleep do you need to feel clear headed and energetic? How many hours in bed are you currently getting? What is your ideal bedtime and rise time? Jot down any tweaks you might like to make.

What gets in the way of good sleep for you? What helps you to sleep well? Jot down three actionable steps or commitments to yourself to promote better sleep.

_____

_____

_____

_____

_____

_____

_____

_____

_____

_____

_____

_____

_____

_____

_____

Pre-bedtime ritual

Keep it consistent – Aim for the same bedtime and rise time each day. While many sleep experts advocate getting to bed by around 10pm, you need to take into consideration your own body clock and daily commitments. See what works best with the demands of your current circumstances and experiment with the windows of time that help you best drift off and wake feeling refreshed.

Digital detox – Aim for at least 30 minutes of screen-free time before bed. The negative effects of electronics on sleep quality are well known, but most adults use some kind of gadget in the hour before bed. If you think that your e-reader helps you unwind, think again! The light emitted causes the same kind of reduction in sleepiness and disruption to your circadian rhythms as other electronics. Read a printed book, or listen to music or an audiobook as an alternative.

Relax your body – Take a bath or shower, or try some calming breath work or gentle yoga.

Relax your mind – If it is swirling with thoughts, try a 'brain dump' and write down any nagging thoughts using a pen and paper. Ask yourself whether these things are as pressing as you first thought. Write down anything you genuinely need to tackle tomorrow so you can let it slip from your mind now. If there are pressing issues that regularly interfere with your ability to relax, reach out and talk to someone.

Prime yourself for sleep – Cue your mind by wearing pyjamas that you love and using soothing scents such as lavender on your body or your pillow.

My ideal pre-bedtime ritual...

Legs up the wall

This is a wonderful practice to slot into your pre-bedtime ritual. Notice how you feel before and after.

Have a cushion and blanket within easy reach.

Sit on the floor with your side towards either the base of a wall or the sofa. Carefully lie on your back and then swing your legs up the wall or on to the sofa. The wall provides a more restorative effect, but can be a strong hamstring stretch, so be guided by your comfort. Place the cushion beneath your head and drape a blanket over you. Stay here for five minutes or more and allow your body to be held. There is nothing to be done but soften and release.

The power of rest

Even when you are getting adequate sleep, the opportunity to stop, rest and relax is a vital part of caring for your health and well-being. Every human needs time where they can just 'be', by which I mean time where there is an absence of striving, effort or problem-solving, and a complete absence of ambition.

Time out allows healing, cleansing and purification to occur, from physiological regeneration on a cellular level to a replenishment of the energy stores on an emotional and psychological level. We often associate the benefits of activities such as yoga with stress management, but it's shown to have tangible positive effects on the immune system as well.

Seeking stillness stimulates growth and cultivates sensitivity. We all need time to regroup and take stock. This quiet reflection helps us to think clearly and make sound decisions that are more in tune with our goals.

Time spent on your own in contemplation opens your eyes to opportunities. It changes your focus so that you can go back to your daily routine with fresh perspective.

Rest puts you back in touch with your body so you know when to push and when to yield – this is a vital part of establishing a healthy balance.

What does rest facilitate in your life? How do you feel when you are well rested and what does this allow you to do or be?

_____

_____

_____

_____

_____

Even when we make all the right healthy choices, there are times in life when good sleep is inaccessible. Be gentle with yourself. Jot down some ways you can be kind to yourself in the aftermath of poor sleep.

_____

_____

_____

_____

_____

Easy meditations to help you unwind

Take a meditative shower – Be present and let the water unwind you. Immerse yourself in the sensation of the water against your skin: connect with the cleansing properties of it, feeling your troubles wash away with the water.

'I am' meditations – You can make this a formal sitting practice, or simply do it while on your commute, at your desk or standing by the kitchen sink. As you breathe in, repeat the words 'I am', and as you breathe out, choose a word that cultivates how you want to feel. I often use words such as: OK, calm, energetic, resourceful, strong, patient, loving, loved, resolute, healthy and blessed. You can keep repeating the one phrase or change with each exhalation. If you prefer, just stick with 'I' on the inhalation and 'am' on the exhalation – that fact is irrefutable.

Seek out beauty – Wherever you are, be on the lookout for something inspiring and uplifting. Beauty lifts your spirits and opens you up to an experience of awe. From your desk at work, maybe it's the cloudscape. Perhaps during your commute to the office or on the school run, you can focus on the trees. Keep a vase of flowers at home to gaze upon. Be aware of artwork around you, and notice architectural beauty too.

Practise yoga nidra – This is a type of guided relaxation. Find a comfy spot and snuggle in.

Rest doesn't have to be lying down in stillness doing nothing. How do you like to recharge? Make a list of the different ways you can top up your energy bank – include some quick fixes that you can dot throughout your day and some longer practices that you might need to make an appointment with yourself to enjoy.

MOVEMENT & NUTRITION

The topics of exercise and nutrition are rich and plentiful grounds for exploration, but for our self-care purposes I want to keep it simple, real and achievable. At the heart of my message here is the recognition that relying on willpower alone is not enough. Welcome to being human – you can stop giving yourself a hard time. We can make up for willpower deficit: first by using strategies to reduce the number of decisions we have to make, and secondly, by using psychological tools to dial down the volume on temptation so our willpower is not so taxed.

Healthy movement

Rather than thinking about exercise, let's aim for movement. Here are some principles of healthy movement:

Aim for 20 minutes of movement daily – It needn't be sport or the gym, and it needn't be punitive. A walk around the block still counts!

Move for mental health – It's not just about rippling abs and toned thighs: movement boosts your clarity of mind and creativity, releases stress and helps you make better decisions.

Keep it varied and keep it fun – Sustainable commitment to daily movement is all about finding a form of exercise that is intrinsically enjoyable to you. Be prepared to think laterally and try lots of different things. Keep your motivation up by varying your exercise routine.

Work with what you've got - You don't need a gym or fancy equipment, all you need is your body! One minute, five minutes, ten minutes – whatever you've got is always better than nothing. Movement has a cumulative effect.

Plan ahead – Know your windows of opportunity and get organized. Research which exercise classes you like, at times that might work for you. Keep spare exercise kit in your car. Make an appointment with yourself if you need to.

List of a few different forms of
movement you can engage in.

_____

_____

_____

_____

_____

_____

Identify windows in your day when you
can get out and move. Make a contract
with yourself by diarizing it or keeping
blank space for you to fill with the
nourishment of your choosing.

_____

_____

_____

_____

_____

_____

Healthy nutritional choices

The key to sustainable healthy eating is to make good choices most of the time. Here are some examples of making healthy and nutritious choices:

1. Fill up on unprocessed foods – fresh and whole – and aim for a wide variety of colours.

2. Work with the 'energy in, energy out' equation if you are aiming to create physical change.

3. Respect your hunger. Get to know it again and really listen to it. Don't let yourself get starving hungry or 'hangry' – this is when you are more likely to make poor food choices.

4. Stop eating when you're full. By eating slowly and mindfully, you have a better chance of gauging when you are full.

5. Acknowledge when you are reaching for food for reasons other than hunger. Remember: we're not just fuelling and hydrating the body, we need to nourish our minds and feed our brains to help us think straight!

What does healthy eating look like for you? Acknowledge what you are doing well and affirm your commitment to those choices. If things need refining, break it down into waves of change. You could look at breakfast, lunch, dinner, snacks or hydration. Jot down your mini action plan and tackle it one step at a time.

_____

_____

_____

_____

_____

_____

_____

_____

_____

_____

_____

Mindful nutrition

One of the easiest ways to bring self-care into your daily life is to turn an existing behaviour into a ritual of nourishment. The way you eat your meals provides a perfect opportunity – you are doing it anyway, so why not attune yourself fully to the sustenance it offers you?

Today, bring mindfulness to your eating and hydration. With everything that passes your lips, bring your full attention to it. This means downing tools, switching off screens and letting your to-do list wait. Follow these steps:

Slow down and tune in to the sensations of hunger and thirst that you feel – Notice the cues from your body and take loving action to feed your mood and fuel your body.

Choose where you will savour your meal – Eating at your desk or in front of the television seldom creates a nourishing experience. Can you go outside or sit somewhere that you find naturally life-giving?

Carefully select what you are going to ingest – Any doubts about what constitutes a healthy choice? Ask your 'Future Self' (you in a few hours from now, tomorrow or a few months down the track – it's up to you). Which nutritional choice will bring you closer to who you aspire to be?

Bring all of your senses to the act of eating and drinking – Notice the colours, the aromas, the textures and flavours and feel the sensation of swallowing.

Notice how much food or drink is required for you to feel satisfied and respect that cue.

Reflect on how this practice went for you.
Observe how it can help you make different
choices and how it facilitates a different
experience of eating and drinking.

_____

_____

_____

_____

_____

_____

_____

_____

_____

_____

_____

_____

_____

_____

_____

Swaps

What are some foods or drinks that you can (relatively painlessly) swap for something else?

For example, for me, coffee is a 'gateway'– I'm tempted to add sugar, and then I want more sugary things, such as cakes and biscuits. Green tea, on the other hand, has me reaching for healthier snack alternatives and keeps sugar cravings at bay. But that's just me. What can you substitute?

Prime your brain: 'If... then'

Anticipate situations that make it hard to stick to healthy food choices and plan how to deal with it. Think about some 'If... then' primer statements for healthy eating and write them down so you're not relying on willpower. So, for example:

- If I'm having a coffee, I'll make it with skimmed milk and no sugar.

- If a friend wants to catch up, then I'll suggest a walk rather than our connection revolving around food.

- If I'm out for dinner and I fancy a dessert, then I will share one.

If I'm..., then I will...

_____

_____

_____

_____

_____

_____

_____

_____

_____

_____

_____

_____

_____

_____

_____

_____

_____

_____

_____

_____

What are your favourite scents? Describe how they make you feel.

_____

_____

_____

_____

_____

_____

_____

_____

_____

_____

_____

_____

_____

_____

_____

_____

_____

Clutter cleansing

The environments you are immersed in at home, at work and during all the transitions in between have a tangible effect on your well-being. Our individual responses to our environments may differ – some people feel at ease in physical mess, while for other people, a tidy house is essential for a 'tidy mind'.

We all have our own 'chaos threshold'. Take the time to open your eyes to how your environment is impinging on or facilitating your mental clarity and vitality. Even if you think a chaotic environment doesn't bother you, notice how clearing the clutter can free up an enormous amount of energy.

Take a close look at the space around you. Look for aspects of your environment that recharge and inspire you, and savour the enjoyment this brings. On the other hand, look for ways in which your environment is draining you, and take action where possible. Can you create more harmony, order or something more energizing for you?

Nurturing the skin you live in

Cast the notion of vanity aside and groom your way to better health. Allow that nourishment to be an assertion of self-worth and notice how tending to your physical body boosts your self-esteem and well-being.

I like to bring this type of self-care into action by looking for daily rituals that I can imbue with the intention to nourish myself. As you wake in the morning, think of one thing that you are looking forward to in your day and let your mind anticipate that for a few breaths. As your feet touch the floor by your bed, give thanks for another day, whatever it holds.

As you prepare for the day, choose an outfit that you feel good in – why not wear things that boost your mood? Cull your wardrobe of items that have the opposite effect.

Use a body lotion that you enjoy the scent of, and massage it mindfully into your limbs, noticing how your body feels, and cultivating gratitude for its physical capabilities.

A spritz of your perfume or a room spray will enhance your posture and encourage you to take a few deep breaths whenever you need a lift.

Choose a handwash you love, making a trip to the bathroom an opportunity for nourishment. Savour the scent.

When you return home, remove your shoes and leave your day behind you. I like to change into a comfortable 'home' outfit. This is not something old from my regular wardrobe that I have relegated as unfit to be seen in: it is something I have chosen specifically for its comfort, and that makes me feel good.

My nourishing rituals are...

Self-care colours

Use colours and their different energetic qualities to nourish you throughout your day. Draw on blues to calm you, greens to refresh you, yellows to uplift you, pinks to soothe you and reds to galvanize you.

Significant places

Where are the places that resonate with you? Are there any particular environments that make you feel alive? Is there a location you like to go to remember someone? This is deeply personal, so reflect on the places that hold the most meaning for you.

If you're unable to physically visit, you can go there in your mind's eye, using all of your senses to imagine what it feels like.

Reflect on the places that hold the most meaning for you...

_____

_____

_____

_____

_____

_____

_____

_____

_____

_____

_____

_____

_____

_____

_____

_____

_____

_____

COPING SKILLS FOR TOUGH TIMES

In challenging times, our thinking often becomes impaired and our inner dialogue can become increasingly intrusive. Using self-care and self-awareness, you can develop the skills you need to navigate times of stress, loss or change. Your body has an innate capacity to restore itself to health. This part of the journal is designed to help you reconnect with this natural ability, by adopting life-giving habits. Essentially, this is about unlocking your self-soothing capacity and learning how to manage your energy.

Signs of stress and burnout

Broadly speaking, stress can be conceived as too much happening at once, and people who are stressed can imagine feeling better once they've got a handle on the challenges they're facing. Burnout can be understood as not having enough in the tank to cope: feeling drained, empty and beyond caring. In a state of burnout, problems can seem insurmountable, and it's difficult to muster up the energy for anything, leaving you feeling increasingly helpless and hopeless. I call it 'energetic bankruptcy'. The danger is we can get used to feeling highly stressed and on the cusp of burnout, accepting it as normal. We need to be vigilant about recognizing the early warning signs like disturbed sleep, constant fatigue or difficulty concentrating, and we have to take notice when compensatory behaviours (such as a reliance on alcohol, sugar and caffeine) creep in.

How does burnout feel?

Physical signs – Feeling tired all the time, even when you've met your sleep needs; greater sensitivity to noise; headaches; palpitations; shortness of breath; muscular pain and tension; difficulty relaxing; supressed immune system and frequent illness; bowel upset; change in appetite; nausea; insomnia.

Emotional signs – Feelings of failure, defeat, detachment and loneliness; loss of motivation and hope; numbing or diminished enjoyment and sense of satisfaction; feeling like you are not your 'normal self'; feeling teary, reactive, irritable, angry, cynical and apathetic.

Mental signs – Indecision; poor concentration and memory; finding it hard to switch off; feeling wired; mind fog; feeling overloaded; anxiety; depression; paranoia.

What are your early warning signs of stress or burnout?

_____

_____

_____

_____

_____

_____

_____

_____

_____

_____

_____

_____

_____

_____

_____

_____

The skills for navigating stress and burnout

Mindfulness – Building the ability to notice what is happening within you, your warning signs, and what is unfolding outside of you, and managing your response. Developing the skill of checking in and taking swift recuperative action.

Connection with your body – Noticing how your body feels, building a language for sensation, hearing messages from your body, and cultivating tenderness towards your body.

The ability to relax – Understanding the difference between tension and relaxation, and being able consciously to release physical tension.

Energy management – The ability to notice your energy levels and to re-energize and lift your mood.

Breathing – Reclaiming the ability to breathe naturally and expansively, helping you come home to yourself, to be your own safe place.

Which of these skills do you have already? Do you need to remind yourself to use them when you spot the early signs of stress? Use the steps on pages 42–43 to help you identify which of these skills you would like to cultivate.

My personal toolkit for navigating stress and burnout...

_____

_____

_____

_____

_____

_____

_____

_____

_____

_____

_____

_____

_____

_____

_____

_____

_____

_____

The mindful check-in

Build the habit of checking in with yourself – head, heart and body – at different intervals during your day. It could be first thing in the morning, as you hop into the car after the school run, as you sit down at your desk, before you take a lunch break, when the 2pm energy slump hits, after dinner, or before bed. The ability to notice where you're at forms the foundation for self-care. The mindful check-in is an opportunity to observe your inner cues like hunger, fatigue, tension or pain, as well as your ability to focus or concentrate, any feelings of loneliness or desire to be alone, or the presence of any particular emotion. Observe without judgement or criticism for a minute (or less if you're time squeezed), setting the intention to lovingly tend to any needs you find.

As you build this practice, what do you learn about yourself – the causes of your stress or burnout, and your warning signs? Over time, can you spot them sooner, take more proactive action and feel more in control?

_____

_____

_____

_____

_____

_____

_____

_____

_____

_____

_____

_____

_____

_____

Managing time with the four 'D's

Often when we are excessively stressed, it feels like there just isn't enough time in the day or week. Try adding the four 'D's to your to-do list:

Do it now – It is important and it must be done by you.

Defer it – You need to do it, but it can wait. Schedule it for later.

Delegate it – It is important, but someone else can do it. Give yourself permission to use this one!

Dump it – It doesn't actually need to be done.

Try chanting the mantra: '*I have all the time I need.*'

Even if you don't believe it, it is better for your nervous system than repeating statements of not having enough time. Try it for yourself and see how you go.

Navigating loss and grief

Mention grief and we immediately conjure up associations of the illness or death of a loved one, a relationship breakdown, divorce, job loss or financial loss. There are many other life circumstances that trigger these feelings and it's important to note that these include positive and self-selected changes too, like a career change, having children, taking retirement or moving abroad. You can grieve for a lost culture, time, place, pursuit or incarnation of you, both real and imagined. Just acknowledging the personal loss in these experiences and validating your feelings can be very healing.

Other types of loss include safety, identity, autonomy and future hopes. It may be helpful to know that for all these experiences, grief is a legitimate and normal response.

If we want to be emotionally healthy, we need to notice our emotions and let them move through us. That's not to say we necessarily have to take action on them – that's our choice. Negating, numbing or distracting ourselves from our emotions is exhausting: it creates stress, pain and tension in our bodies and disconnects us from living responsively in the moment. We can numb ourselves to our feelings, but we can't do this selectively, so if we avoid the painful ones, we numb ourselves to the joyful ones too. The healthy solution is to feel what we feel and respond with mindfulness and compassion.

Gratitude, appreciation, awe and admiration

Beneath feelings of loss, we have a great reservoir of thanks and love to mine. Allow your mind to linger on what it is that you loved so much about what's come to pass – the moments, the memories, the lessons, the qualities. In time to come, you may find that your pain is transformed into these emotions, allowing you to wholeheartedly embrace life in its new shape.

Time for reflection

Take some time to think about how you define yourself and reflect on the interconnectedness of life. Find a bench to sit on and watch the hum of life around you. Observe with all your senses: take in the aromas, the sounds, the sights, the tastes and the textures, and notice the memories these evoke.

Let it all wash over you, noticing the movement of people around you – people like you, sitting and watching the world go by, acknowledging your shared experience.

Notice people walking, running, driving, or sitting on buses, trains or planes. Reflect on the times you've taken those modes of transport and the places you've been, connecting with that feeling of common purpose.

Notice the goings-on around you without judgement, and think about when you've had similar experiences. Feel that deep sense of shared humanity, and let your mind linger on the notion that you, like every human being, are an integral part of this whole picture. See how it feels to rely less on things outside of you to define you.

Write a letter to yourself. What do you want
to say to yourself? What do you need
to hear?

_____

_____

_____

_____

_____

_____

_____

_____

_____

_____

_____

_____

_____

_____

_____

Practice to soothe – meditation on your heart centre

Come into a comfortable position with your spine elongated, on a chair or a meditation cushion. Close your eyes, soften the muscles of your face and shoulders and take a few relaxed breaths. As you breathe in, take your fingertips to touch behind the base of your skull, then exhale and slowly move them forwards around your head, without actually touching your head, meeting at the centre of your forehead, palms touching. Breathe in here, and then slowly move your hands to be in front of your heart, keeping the palms together in prayer shape. As you repeat this hand action, imbue it with the intention to gather your mental energy at the centre

of your forehead and bring it down into your heart. You may even begin to feel a sense of energy or warmth between your hands as you press them together, and you may have a sense of this energy moving into your heart centre. After a few minutes, pause with your hands one on top of the other across your heart. Breathe into them and imagine your heart centre as a ball of white light, a candle burning or the sun rising over the ocean. Let your mind's eye linger on this image of light and the feeling of warmth emanating from your heart. Breathe in more light and life and exhale away what you no longer need. Use the mantra: *I can be there for myself*.

TIMELINE OF GRIT

Plot a timeline of your life events – Review your achievements and include the storms you have weathered. How would anyone walking in your shoes feel?

Look to the positive – What qualities do you appreciate about yourself?

Reflect on your current situation – What are you currently doing well? Praise not only positive outcomes but also effort, tenacity, grit, showing up, persistence or care.

Explore your fears – Acknowledge why they are concerns for you. When do you feel at ease and why? Our ability to relax is more than just our muscle fibres: it is also found in congruence, that feeling of peace when we are aligned with our values. Use this information to reflect on what you feel your purpose is.

Make a commitment – Ensure you honour what's important to you, including looking after yourself. What might that commitment look like?

Decisions, decisions...

In forging a new path, you may encounter myriad decisions. If you're facing a choice overload, see if you can reduce the number of options to get a clearer feel for the right one, or simply decrease the number of choices you need to make right now. Do this in partnership with a friend if it feels overwhelming, or go for a brisk walk and see if that brings greater clarity.

Rather than feeling there is a 'right' or 'wrong' decision, acknowledge that there can be several congruent options. It's not about making the one right choice: aim for a 'good' choice. How do you know it's a good choice? It will be harmonious with your values and it will draw on your strengths. You will also feel it in your body. When you're at peace with a choice, you'll sense it in your belly and your breath. If there is discord, your body will let you know, so listen to that gut feeling.

If you feel stuck in indecision, it might help to set some timeframes and use these prompts:

- If I take this option, what are the benefits?

- If I don't take this path, what will I lose?

- How will I feel if I don't do this?

- What's motivating me? Is it fear, doubt, the inner critic, or is it hope, insight or courage?

- If a friend was facing the same choice, what would I advise them to do?

LESSONS IN
SELF-CARE

The best thing about a journal is that you can be honest about what works for you and tailor your own self-care toolkit to have by your side, ready for when you need to top up your energy bank, prioritize rest and relaxation when you are feeling overwhelmed, or get back on the healthy track when your fitness takes a nosedive.

What are the lessons in self-care that you wish to take forward in everyday life? What kind of person does self-care allow you to be? What kind of dreams does it allow you to dream, and then make happen?

Micro-moments of nourishment

Self-care needn't involve large investments of time. Take the 'micro-moments of nourishment' approach and dot them through your day: sixty seconds of being with the breath; savouring the scent of your morning coffee; repeating a mantra to cultivate how you want to feel; a few minutes to unwind at your desk; ten minutes of soothing yoga or journalling before you go to bed. The practices in this book are potent stress-busters and will change the quality of your day, just like hitting the reboot button.

Become skilled in the arts of mindfulness, curiosity, kindness, compassion and savouring: this will transform the lens through which you see the world. In this way, we imbue everyday actions with a feeling of tenderness and care. What are you already doing that you can make more nourishing? The way you greet the day, the way in which you dress yourself, how you shower, how you eat your meals, the way you talk to yourself: these are all things we can turn into a ritual of nourishment with awareness and choice.

What are your favourite micro-moments of nourishment?

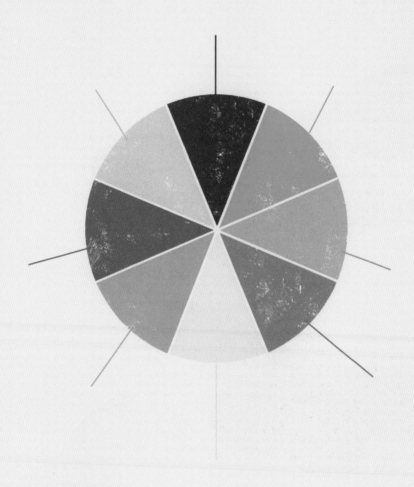

Ask your 'future self' – what do you need to become the person you aspire to be?

Your whole life is a journey of becoming. Without putting any pressure on yourself, imagine your 'future best self'. What kind of choices do they make? How do they talk to themselves and others? How do they spend their time?

Mantra: 'I give myself permission to...'

Ever notice yourself saying 'I shouldn't feel like this' or 'I mustn't think this way'? This mantra is about respecting there is a time and place for all emotions. It's not the presence of emotion that's the problem, it's what we do with it that counts. It is also about helping you fine-tune your inner awareness so you can take action to meet your needs before energetic bankruptcy hits or resentment boils over into toxic behaviour. This mantra will help you bring the skill of mindfulness and your values into daily action. Here are some examples of how you might complete the phrase:

- I give myself permission to feel this loss. I'll sit with it like a friend for the next ten minutes and just let it be.

- I give myself permission to say 'no' to a friend's invitation.

- I give myself permission to say 'yes' to that invitation!

- I give myself permission to switch off and observe a digital detox this weekend.

- I give myself permission to have an early night.

- I give myself permission to dream big and let the 'how' come later.

- I give myself permission to take a break from worry and problem-solving for the next hour. Replenishing my energy bank will help me be more creative later.

- I give myself permission to stand firm and honour my boundaries.

- I give myself permission to speak my truth.

I give myself permission to...

_____

_____

_____

_____

_____

_____

_____

_____

_____

_____

_____

_____

_____

_____

_____

_____

_____

_____

_____

Blue sky mind

Find a comfortable place to sit or lie down; this can be inside or outside, wherever you feel completely at ease.

Close your eyes and just become aware. Feel your body, feel your breathing and notice your mind. Let all these thoughts, emotions, sensations and memories arise as they will. Don't resist them, don't engage with them: just notice them.

Imagine in your mind's eye a big blue sky. Every time a thought, emotion, sensation or memory arises, let it become a cloud in the sky, floating away until the next one comes along.

You are not your thoughts, emotions or sensations: you are the wide blue sky. Relax into that knowledge, staying here for a few minutes, peacefully watching the clouds as they come and go.

Make an appointment with yourself today

We book our car in for a service without guilt: similarly, schedule time in for you.

If self-care is constantly getting bumped, carve out time in the diary and make it a non-negotiable. There is rarely a 'good' time: we need to make time. Whether it is an art class, a session with your osteopath or planning a date night to feed your relationship, give your nourishment the priority it deserves and book it in today.

MY SELF-CARE TOOLKIT

Humans thrive on certainty, so even if you can't guarantee a particular outcome to a challenge you are facing, having a toolkit of things to try can be a powerful coping strategy. Think along the lines of: 'If X happens, then I will Y...' These primer statements become even more powerful when written down. Creating this toolkit can diminish anxiety and will help you take swift, constructive action when challenges arise.e.

- If I am feeling low, then I will use my journal to reflect on my goals.

- If I am feeling fatigued, then I will stand up tall and take six 'mountain breaths' (see page 17).

- If I am feeling time-poor, then I will repeat: 'I have all the time I need.'

- If I am feeling anxious, then I will smooth out my breathing and relax any physical tension I find.

- If I am feeling lonely, then I will scan through who's on my team and reach out to someone.

- If I am feeling reactive, then I will seek out nature and take a moment to enjoy its beauty.

- If I am feeling scattered, then I will focus on my 'why'.

- If I am feeling bored, then I will think about something I am looking forward to.

- If I am feeling fed up, then I will take a walk around the block to let off steam.

- If I am feeling happy, then I will savour it!

If I am feeling low, then I will...

_____

If I am feeling fatigued, then I will...

_____

If I am feeling time-poor, then I will...

_____

If I am feeling anxious, then I will...

_____

If I am feeling lonely, then I will...

_____

If I am feeling reactive, then I will...

_____

If I am feeling scattered, then I will...

_____

If I am feeling bored, then I will...

_____

If I am feeling fed up, then I will...

_____

If I am feeling happy, then I will...

_____

Author's note

Thank you for journeying with me here. While you may have reached the final pages, we're not done yet – but do give yourself a pat on the back for the investments in your well-being that you've already made. Just by reading this journal you have planted the seeds for growth and nourishment.

Our needs and preferences are constantly changing, so our self-care practices also need to evolve. Keep dipping into this journal: something new might catch your eye or an old insight might just drop in deeper. We create sustainable change in incremental waves, so use this journal to keep refining your daily habits. This is how we transform our lives – one habit at a time. It is such a joy to learn and grow together. I am cheering you on.

Suz xx

P.S. Come and be a part of my caring community on Instagram – Monday live sessions at 9am! We're walking the path together.

My notes

Picture credits